Advanced
Cursive Handwriting Practice
Workbook for Teens

Julie Harper

Advanced Cursive Handwriting Practice Workbook for Teens

Copyright © 2016 Julie Harper

Cover Design by Melissa Stevens
www.theillustratedauthor.net
Write. Create. Illustrate.

Teens > Education & Reference > Language Arts

ISBN 10: 1523234598

EAN 13: 978-1523234592

Table of Contents

Introduction

Compared to Julie Harper's original Cursive Handwriting Practice Workbook for Teens, this workbook is "advanced" in the following ways:

- ✓ It uses a smaller font size.
- ✓ The blank lines are narrower.
- ✓ There is just a quick refresher of basic letter and word practice.
- ✓ Most pages aren't designed to be traced prior to copying.
- ✓ A challenge chapter includes visual exercises.
- ✓ The last chapter includes creative writing prompts.

The goal of this workbook is to inspire teens' interest in learning and practicing cursive handwriting. Teens enjoy reading and writing sentences they can relate to like, "Set your alarm to play your favorite song." Exercises like these help to make learning fun, whether in the classroom or at home.

Students who need more practice writing individual letters or single words may benefit from using this workbook in combination with a basic cursive writing workbook which focuses on more basic techniques.

May your students or children improve their handwriting skills and enjoy reading and writing these teenage-oriented sentences and paragraphs.

Uppercase Cursive Alphabet

$\mathcal{A}$ $\mathcal{B}$ $\mathcal{C}$ $\mathcal{D}$ $\mathcal{E}$ $\mathcal{F}$

$\mathcal{G}$ $\mathcal{H}$ $\mathcal{I}$ $\mathcal{J}$ $\mathcal{K}$ $\mathcal{L}$

$\mathcal{M}$ $\mathcal{N}$ $\mathcal{O}$ $\mathcal{P}$ $\mathcal{Q}$ $\mathcal{R}$

$\mathcal{S}$ $\mathcal{T}$ $\mathcal{U}$ $\mathcal{V}$ $\mathcal{W}$ $\mathcal{X}$

$\mathcal{Y}$ $\mathcal{Z}$

♫ ᵥ ♫

Lowercase Cursive Alphabet

a   b   c   d   e   f

g   h   i   j   k   l

m   n   o   p   q   r

s   t   u   v   w   x

y   z

Part 1 Quick Letter Review

Part 1 Instructions: Copy the letters and words onto the blank line below.

Aa Aa – Adagio artist Audience abstract Awesome audio

Bb Bb – Breakdance blues Ballroom ballet Bunny best

Cc Cc – Charleston chicken Clog cha-cha Choreography cell

Dd Dd – Dance disco Diva dreamy Dress diary Drive

Ee Ee – Entertainment electric Expressive e-mail Exit

Ff Ff – Fandango fly Flamenco foxtrot Favorite friend

Gg Gg – Gangnam guide Game gorgeous Genius go

Hh Hh – Hustle harmony Hammer-time hula Hip-hop

Ii Ii – Interpretive ideal Inquire ironic Imagine ink

Jj Jj – Jazz jig Jump jam Journey jest Jockey jewel

Kk Kk – Karma kiss Kidding karate Kung Fu knot

_____

_____

Ll Ll – Lambada line Leotard lift Leap lazy Likely

_____

_____

Mm Mm – Macarena mambo Music moves Motion

_____

_____

Nn Nn – Nice neon Never nudge Nature nautical No way

_____

_____

Oo Oo – Original out Obvious ooze Organic once Oh man

_____

_____

Pp Pp – Pokey pop Paradise play Phone practice Power

_____

_____

Qq Qq – Quick quest Quality quiet Quote quite Queen

Rr Rr – Robot rock Reggae radio Rehearsal run Rhythm

Ss Ss – Shuffle song Scheming star Sound steps Show

Tt Tt – Tango twist Tune theatre Technique tempo Talent

Uu Uu – Ultra universal Unique uneven Upgrade usual

Vv Vv – Vogue visual Valentine vanilla Vibrant violet

Ww Ww – Waltz wild Whimsy who What when Where

Xx Xx – Xylophone x-ray Xenon xvi X-tra xyz

Yy Yy – Yoga you Youthful yes Yeah yacht Year young

Zz Zz – Zumba zany Zing zebra Zone zillion Zeal zoo

ABC DEF GHI JKL MNO PQR STU VWX YZ

ab cd ef gh ij kl mn op qr st uv wx yz

♫ // ♫

Aa – Adept acting always amazes an audience

Bb – Best buddies bounce big brown basketballs

Cc – Chill, cool, confident, calm, and collected

Dd – Delicious, delectable double-dipped donut

Ee – Enthusiastic, energetic, and eager entertainers

Ff – Favorite fun friends are forever fantastic

Gg – Glamorous, glittery, glitzy, and gorgeous

Hh – Hot, hip, humorous, and hearty hashtags

Ii – Impressive, imaginative, and inspiring ideas

Jj – Jealous juvenile juggling while jaywalking

Kk – Kind kisses amid karaoke and kaleidoscopes

Ll – Laugh loud, live long, and love life

Mm – Merrily move to mysterious mandolin music

Nn – Neon necklaces naturally get noticed at night

Oo – Outstanding occasions often occur outside

Pp – Pepperoni, red pepper, and pineapple on pizza

Qq – Quit quarreling over quiz questions

Rr – Refreshing, restful, and relaxing at the river

Ss — Secret, sweet, and special surprises seem surreal

_____

_____

Tt — Teenagers text and type tweets with their tablets

_____

_____

Uu — Unrecognized unicorns under used umbrellas

_____

_____

Vv — Valentines love visiting villages with vivid views

_____

_____

Ww — Who? What? When? Where? Why? How?

_____

_____

Xx — Exercise through kickboxing and boxing

_____

_____

Yy - Yearn for yummy, yummy yellow yogurt

Zz - Zap zombies zooming through the zany maze

Absolutely beautiful, courageous, daring, eager friends glimpsed

hilarious independent jumping kangaroos looking mighty

nervous overlooking playful, quickly running stallions trying

to understand various wacky, x-treme youthful zebras.

Part 2 Letter Blends

Part 2 Instructions: Copy the letters and words onto the blank line below.

ab ab – caboose jab absent cabin table ability grab amiable

ac ac – backpack academics stacked package accept fireplace

ad ad – fad admire read graduate mad carload radar tread

af af – café afraid craft deafen loafer after taffy waffle raft

ag ag — teenager magazine tag agonize brag pageant stage

ai ai — braid lair airplane train fair maintain vain explain

ak ak — break freakish mistake shaking cloak squeak quake

al al — mall musical casual male female almost dialog rally

am am — gamer slam team among blame jamboree famous

an an — dance groan answer danger maniac analyze trance

ap ap – rap adaptor shape capsize cape relapse leap apply

ar ar – party artist scary smart garage dark compare share

at at – Saturday date attendance eat catch math feat what

aw aw – awful draw straw jaw claw takeaway saw dawn

ba ba – band basketball baseball bat abandon tuba payback

bb bb – dribble bubble fibber robber gobble dubbing grabbed

be be — maybe better beast chamber label strobe beat beach

bi bi — bit binary exhibit alibi habit binder birthday cabin

bl bl — blog blast ablaze double trouble mumble blink blue

bo bo — keyboard boom limbo about lifeboat body boast bored

br br — vibrant library braid fabric abroad branch brink

bu bu — busy abundant buy busted abuzz bummer burp

by by – byte ruby baby lullaby byline hobby abysmal

ca ca – macarena scare castle educate academy calm cassette

cc cc – accept succeed occupy zucchini broccoli accent occur

ce ce – dancer recently ace decent graceful face juice excel farce

ch ch – beach munch charm enrich chimney chess checkers

ci ci – facial excite circle accident city authenticity science

ck ck – backpack luck quick stuck heckle paycheck truck rock

cl cl – school clone circle obstacle enclosure recliner cycle clever

co co – recording cool falcon disco escort scold helicopter cocoa

cq cq – acquainted racquet lacquer acquiring acquittal

cr cr – crush crafty acrobat script micro describe crew screech

cy cy – fancy juicy motorcycle mercy unicycle cyclone

da da — dancing date danger bandage medal cheddar dare

dd dd — addition puddle muddy ruddy odd bladder saddle

de de — garden deep collide indent defender pretended decoy

dg dg — pledge badger judging ridges dodged abridged lodging

di di — disc divide cardiac diamond editing idiotic dissect dish

do do — tuxedo doomed dormitory corridor abandon dodo

dr dr — dream draw kindred wondrous backdrop drill dreary

ee ee — tweet cheeky degree exceed peek week sweet jeep wheel

eg eg — college ego beg allege begin regret peg leg vegan eggs

eq eq — equal sequel sequin unequal require equidistant request

ex ex — explore complex flex vex expel hex index expire

fa fa — fame face familiar alfalfa infamous farce sofa fact

fe fe – café festival curfew life forfeit referee fear feelings female

ff ff – dandruff fluffy puffy spiffy affair buffer offer buffy

fi fi – infinity film finest definitive fight figure pacifist fib

fl fl – flaming fleece flagpole inflated afloat flag flight flex

fr fr – freckle friend frozen afraid freedom afresh fried saffron

fu fu – fun function helpful dreadful fuming fusion funny

fy fy – goofy iffy identify clarify rectify gratify unify defy

ga ga – games gaze vulgar arrogant legal garage organ toga

ge ge – age general change abridge blockage cottage gesture edge

gg gg – blogger giggle jogging shaggy egg digging wiggle rugged

gh gh – ghost fright eighteen laughter delightful aghast rightly

gi gi – imagine girls gigantic allergic logical agility gigabyte

gl gl — glow dangling eyeglasses glitter angle bugle glide glee

go go — google goad gossip gorgeous agonize category ego Gothic

gr gr — fragrance graphics hungry groove agree grab gravity

gy gy — gymnasium gypsy apology biology strategy gyrate

ha ha — hashtag chat harmony shave harp behave sharing

he he — theater she her cheer heat hex where help phenomenal

hi hi — hits hip his him higher achieve hike chisel think ship

hu hu — hunk chuckle hush brochure chunk human hug

hy hy — hype shy hydrate physics scratchy stretchy hybrid

ia ia — social media facial initial diarrhea criteria material

ie ie — movie jazziest craziest brainier achiever glacier pier

ig ig — design bright igloo big align neighbor fatigue highest

iv iv — vivid active ivy river alive quiver activate giving

ix ix — sixteen mixed affix suffix fixture mixture six fixed

ja ja — jazz jam jade ajar hijack jaywalk jacket jamboree

je je — jewelry jeans jeer jealousy jelly jet jerk jeep jello jester

ji ji — jinx jingle jittery jigsaw jitterbug jiu-jitsu jiggle jibe

jo jo — joke enjoy jolly major adjourned join joy job jock

ju ju – junior juicy judge unjustly adjust juxtapose juggle

ka ka – karaoke karma kaleidoscope kayak skating kazoo

ke ke – weekend keyboard hike attacked breaker keepsake

ki ki – kiss skin bikini biking kidding kingly kindness skid

kk kk – knickknack trekking trekkers trekked bookkeeper

kn kn – knight known acknowledge sickness knowledge

ko ko – workout cookout hickory reckon koala koi

_____

_____

ky ky – skyline rocky yucky cheeky finicky silky sky

_____

_____

la la – cellular chocolate lady slam balance play blame

_____

_____

le le – style dilemma male female allergic leap wiggle fable

_____

_____

lg lg – algebra algae tailgate vulgar divulges pilgrim

_____

_____

li li – chili blister likelihood limited deliver helicopter like list

_____

_____

ll ll – chill ball doll scroll llama fill allow all falling call

_____

_____

lu lu – slumber clumsy fluid blunder blue clueless lunch

_____

_____

ma ma – magician smart master maniacal man woman

_____

_____

mb mb – zombie ambiance rumble mumble climb mambo

_____

_____

me me – aflame blame frame member kismet fame time

_____

_____

mi mi – mighty admittance ceramic emit optimism mine

_____

_____

mm mm – summer clammy mammal plummet simmer

my my – mystical dreamy steamy academy army creamy

na na – naughty inane culinary finality analysis banana

nd nd – sound band sand bland abandon brand ending

ne ne – cologne designer never bone panel kinetic one trainer

ni ni – nightly ignite banister animal definite nine feminine

nn nn – annoy cinnamon scanner banner penny dinner

no no – noise abnormal know snore ignore donor snooze

ny ny – funny nylon anonymous anyone botany shiny

oa oa – moat oak boat float carload goad overboard goals

of of – goof off often tofu soften aloof proof lofty offer roof

og og – blogging dialog doghouse jogger soggy noggin analogy

oi oi – voice moisten loiter poise join spoiler oil noise toil

oo oo – ooze goofy oodles moody book look proof cook shook

os os – pose rosy frost glossy hospital osmosis mostly almost

ot ot – photo shoot boots knotted both egotist cotton mother

pa pa – paradise topaz sparkle pampered impact parade

pe pe – chaperon desperate special expel inspect repeat pepper

ph ph – phone photograph nephew phrase phony physique

pi pi – picturesque cupid piano pimple perspire aspiring pity

pl pl – play plural explode replica splinter crumple plug

pp pp – zippy happy puppy approval oppose wrapped

pr pr – prom praise spring culprit impress expressive proud

pu pu – purple compute spunky purse spurt put puny

py py – pyramid copy therapy canopy occupy grumpy

ra ra – attraction trance fragrance race raisin dragnet trap

re re – stereo retro red remember conspire stream retire redo

ri ri – riddle hysterical describe florist crimson pride gripe

rr rr – horror terror starring carrier arrest starry barrage

ru ru – ruby cherub trust bruise disrupt brunch cruel truce

ry ry – wizardry artistry blistery very entry hurry hungry

sa sa – rehearsal lasagna essay disaster refusal sale insanity

se se – poise season consent rehearse sender wise praise

si si – music sister vision position allusion classify sign

sk sk – risky ski skate whisker mask askew sketch sky skit

sl sl – island sleep famously slippery aisle slap slinky

sm sm — smoothly cosmetic smart charisma spasm smile

sn sn — sneaky snafu parsnip snap snooze snow snacks

so so — social blossom somewhere absorb liaison insomnia

ss ss — scissors dessert bass assist glossy bossy crisscross

su su — summer pleasure casual sugar insult sure suntan

ta ta — guitar fantasy mistaken pita distant tango tape

te te – cute tease test write note teammates taste jittery

ti ti – attitude time exciting timid tiny stink action tired

to to – photography toner cartoon tomorrow top into too

tr tr – theatrical instrument truck strength trust track

tt tt – twitter glittery flutter buttery rotten cottage mittens

tw tw – twilight tweet twice twinge between twelve twisted

uk uk – jukebox fluke lukewarm ukulele puke duke nukes

un un – unique sunny fun tunes pun unsung pungent

ur ur – journey purse allure burgundy curse azure ours

va va – vacation variety values valid vast vanity

vo vo – vogue voice vote evolve volition favorable avoid

wa wa – cakewalk beware await waste want wackiest

wh wh – whistle cartwheel awhile why whoa wheelie whom

wi wi – wish wisdom citywide freewill twinkle swinging

wl wl – crawl bowl prowl owl yawl growling awl fowl

wo wo – wonderful two worldly keyword powwow words

ws ws – curfews drowsy windows fellows arrows shows

za za – pizza zapped plaza zigzag sizable bizarre hazard

Part 3 Write Sentences

Part 3 Instructions: Copy each sentence onto the blank line below.

Zumba makes fitness seem like a dance party.

_____

_____

Hips move fast and wide during the macarena.

_____

_____

Feet turn into drums when you tap dance.

_____

_____

Jazz up your style with dramatic bold movements.

_____

_____

Couples spin and jump together in swing dancing.

_____

_____

Partners engage in a complex dance when they tango.

_____

_____

Stories are told through the dance and music of ballet.

_____

_____

Dance freestyle while listening to hip-hop music.

_____

_____

Flamenco combines singing, dancing, and guitar together.

_____

_____

Can you breakdance, do the twist, or do the robot?

_____

_____

Listen to your playlist and tune out the world.

Relax and enjoy your favorite songs.

Sing like you are singing in front of a full stadium.

Music is an expression of your inner feelings.

Sing in the shower. Sing in the car. Sing all day.

Sing in the rain. Sing in the sunshine.

Dance to your favorite song.

Dancing is contagious. Catch it and have fun.

Feel the freedom of your movements while dancing.

Your worries are forgotten while you are dancing.

Stop and dance. It doesn't cost anything to dance.

Be bold! Dance while everybody is watching.

Listen to the pulsating beat of the music.

Set your alarm to play your favorite song.

Start the day by singing along to that special song.

Sing and escape into your own musical world.

You feel like you will never tire of hearing your favorite song.

Life wouldn't seem complete without music.

Think outside not only the box, but the whole city, too.

How? Go camping and enjoy the great outdoors.

Find the perfect fishing hole. Catch and release.

Get close to nature and be a happy camper.

Spend time with friends around the campfire.

Roast marshmallows, hot dogs, and S'mores.

Pick your favorite sport. Push yourself to your limits.

_____

Gymnastics is my life. I can stick it.

_____

I dig volleyball. Let's meet at the net.

_____

Dive in and swim like a fish. I love the water.

_____

Skateboarding is both my sport and my transportation.

_____

Horseback ride in the country, and feel the freedom.

_____

Baseball is our national pastime. It's my game.

Football players go for the goal. It's the longest 100 yards.

Hockey is my love. Meet me on the frozen pond.

I live to dribble and shoot hoops. Play basketball.

Tennis is my passion. I love to serve tennis balls.

I would rather be teeing it up on the golf course.

Let's hit the slopes and ski in the great beyond.

Cheerleading is a sport for the very energetic.

Extreme sports are for the daring. They know no limits.

Water polo brings the action to the swimming pool.

Enjoy the simple pleasure of bike riding.

When you play softball, it's okay to steal a base.

Overcome obstacles. Cross the finish line.

I can compete against myself when I run.

Leave your snowboard marks on the fresh snow.

Train hard. Leave your worries at the gym.

Weightlifters know that no pain is no gain.

Professional auto racers have a need for speed.

Be a team player, and don't go it alone. Go, team!

Whatever your sport, enjoy playing it. Team spirit!

Give it your best, and you will be a winner inside.

It takes dedication and teamwork to be a winner.

Train and play hard, but don't forget to have fun.

Win or lose, always be a good sport.

Which kinds of movies do you prefer to watch?

_____

_____

Do you like ghosts, vampires, werewolves, or zombies?

_____

_____

Do you enjoy a romantic comedy?

_____

_____

Do you prefer movies that are dramatic or humorous?

_____

_____

Do you like movies packed with action and adventure?

_____

_____

Who is your favorite actor or actress?

_____

_____

What is the title of your favorite book?

_____

_____

What is the name of your favorite author?

_____

_____

What genres and subjects do you prefer to read?

_____

_____

Do you prefer hardback, paperback, or digital books?

_____

_____

How many books do you read each year?

_____

_____

Which do you enjoy more: a good book or movie?

_____

_____

Snap a picture of you, your friends, or the scenery.

_____

_____

Taking pictures helps to preserve the good times.

_____

_____

Always keep your memories close to your heart.

_____

_____

Smile or pout. Goofy face. Duck face. Funny hat.

_____

_____

It's fun and easy to customize and edit your photos.

_____

_____

Share your memories with family and friends.

_____

_____

Best friends help make your life beautiful.

Surround yourself with good friends.

A true friend accepts and loves who you are.

Friends know how to help you reach for the stars.

Support your friends and always be there for them.

Be a good listener, but stop gossip before it spreads further.

Enjoy a warm summer day at the beach.

Soak up the sun, but don't forget the sunscreen.

Ride the waves, run in the sand, or create sand art.

Toss a Frisbee and play volleyball with your friends.

What are your favorite snacks to enjoy at the beach?

Explore the beach for seashells.

Spend the day at an amusement park with your friends.

Wait in line to ride the scariest roller coaster. Whee!

Gently crash into one another in bumper cars.

Get soaked on a water ride on a hot summer day.

Enjoy snacks: cotton candy, hot dogs, and popcorn.

Splurge on a souvenir to remember the fun day.

Enjoy the moment. Laugh out loud.

Sometimes it takes courage to follow your heart.

You make a difference with the choices you make.

Always be yourself. Don't change just to please another.

Believe and know that your dreams can come true.

Always remember that you are that shining star.

It's okay to hug your teddy bear.

_____

Teen crush! Girl crush! Boy crush!

_____

Your voice and opinion are important.

_____

You do have an impact on the future.

_____

Reach for the stars. They are within your reach.

_____

All stars shine in the darkness.

_____

Be happy. Please yourself. Just be yourself. Simple as that.

Turn a frown upside down to make a smile.

Smile. It's free, and can ease tension. Nature's ice-breaker.

Happiness is having a forever friend. Best friends forever!

Surround yourself with positive personalities.

Reach for your dreams because you can do it. Yes, you can!

Part 4 Write Paragraphs

Part 4 Instructions: Copy each paragraph onto the blank lines below.

Dance any dance. Pick your favorite dance. Dance by yourself in front of a full-length mirror.

A dancer is an artist and an athlete. Dance your way through life. Dance to be you. Dance your troubles away.

Note: You should have enough room below to skip every other line.

Find your fitness... Is it body building on the beach, enjoying yoga and meditation, running in a marathon, basketball, football, softball, gymnastics, dancing, cheerleading, swimming, skateboarding, bicycling, wrestling, ballet, surfing, swimming, hockey, soccer, mountaineering, snow skiing, water skiing, tennis, or one of the martial arts?

Bike riding is good for the heart and the soul. It also allows you to avoid traffic jams.

Pedaling your mountain bike up winding pathways leads you to amazing views of the beauty of nature. The view at the top of the mountain is even sweeter.

Keep pedaling.

Let's have an ice-cream social. If you serve Neapolitan ice-cream, you will be scooping three of the four most popular ice-cream flavors. Add a banana, nuts, and whipped cream to the vanilla, chocolate, and strawberry ice-cream to make a banana split. It will surely be a sweet time for you and all of your friends.

Can you imagine not having a cell phone? The first mobile phone weighed over two pounds. The large and heavy battery took about ten hours to charge, and gave less than thirty minutes of talk time. Initially, they were only used to talk, and voicemail wasn't even available. Text messaging became available in the early nineties.

Invite a date to the prom. Shop for your tuxedo or dress. Traditionally, a corsage is placed on the girl's wrist. Dance with your date to a slow song. Enjoy punch and cake. Have fun with all your friends. Listen to music. Dance, dance, dance. Share stories with friends. Savor these moments so you can remember them for a lifetime.

How many silly words do you know? Bugaboo is a source of great distress. Cattywampus is disarray. Jabberwocky is meaningless speech. Bumfuzzled is perplexed. Widdershins is counterclockwise. Funambulist is a tightrope walker. Befuddle is to confuse. Popinjay is conceited. Hodgepodge is a confused mixture.

It's time to make a splash and have a pool party. Have guests bring towels and swim suits. Pass out water balloons and squirt guns. Serve chips and lemonade.

Organize pool games. Dive down to the bottom for prizes. Float like jellyfish. Play Marco Polo.

Remember to take time out for floating on a raft.

Do you enjoy shopping at the mall?

If so, what are your favorite stores? What kinds of things do you like to shop for?

If not, what don't you like about it? What do you prefer to do instead?

When was the last time you visited a mall?

_____
_____
_____
_____
_____
_____
_____
_____
_____
_____
_____
_____

Imagine spending Halloween night in a supposedly haunted hotel with friends and family. You could explore the grounds together. You could research the hotel's history. You could watch a horror movie. You could stay up late telling scary ghost stories. What a frightening Halloween that would be, especially if you saw a real ghost. Too scary?

When you visit a movie theater, which kinds of movies do you enjoy watching? Do you like horror, comedy, romance, suspense, action, or something else?

Do you like to eat popcorn, nachos, or candy while you watch the movie? Do you like to sip a drink?

What was the last movie that you watched?

Just write. Pound away at your keyboard. Let the words flow. Listen to your inner muse. Be creative.

Challenge yourself with rhythm or rhyme in a poem, tell a tale with a short story, or crank out an adventure in a novel. Develop new characters and watch them grow right before your eyes. Create a whole new world.

Do you ever practice making faces in front of the mirror?

It can be fun.

When your reflection smiles, it can help cheer you up. See if you can make a pouty face (just for fun). How does your angry face look? Try out a sigh. Give yourself a smirk. Don't forget to make a silly face.

Did you know that coloring isn't just for kids? Millions of adults are now into adult coloring books. They serve as a fun and creative way to relieve stress. Teens can enjoy them, too. You can even organize a teenage coloring book party. Everyone needs the same book. (It's not too expensive when everyone buys their own.) Then you can have a coloring contest.

Collecting can be a fun hobby.

You can collect just about anything: coins, souvenirs, bottle caps, antiques, stuffed animals, knickknacks, vintage clothing, and so much more.

Have you ever collected anything? If so, what was it?

If not, why haven't you?

Challenge yourself by seeing what you and your friends know. How many of the fifty states (of the United States) can you write down in ten minutes? How many U.S. presidents can you remember? How many elements from the periodic table can you name from the symbols? How many classic books can you name?

Part 5 Challenge Exercises

Part 5 Note: This chapter is intended to provide a fun and challenging diversion for those students who may enjoy such exercises. If these exercises don't appeal to you, feel free to move onto the next chapter.

Instructions: First trace each sentence. Then try writing each sentence in the space provided. It may be handy to use a pencil with a good eraser.

See if you can write up and down this staircase.

This sentence makes a sudden right turn.

First climb up the hill, and then slide to the bottom.

Welcome to the valley of cursive handwriting.

Surf's up. Ride the word waves. The water's nice.

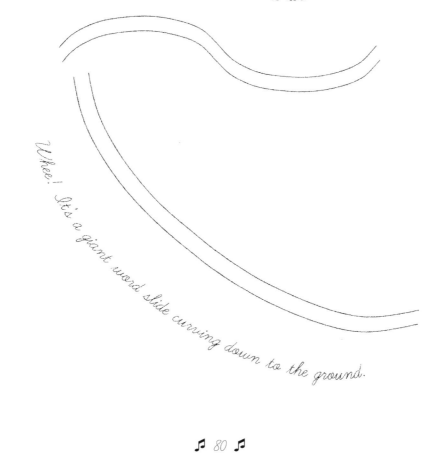

Whee! It's a giant word slide curving down to the ground.

♫ 80 ♫

Write along the three sides of this equilateral triangle. Turn the book upside down.

Think outside the square in order to write inside of it.

This square doesn't seem so boring, does it? A fun square.

Are word diamonds also a girl's best friend, or just real diamonds? Well, word diamonds aren't a thing...

Be confident. You're done! Dance around this six-sided hexagon. Rotate the book as you read and write this paragraph.

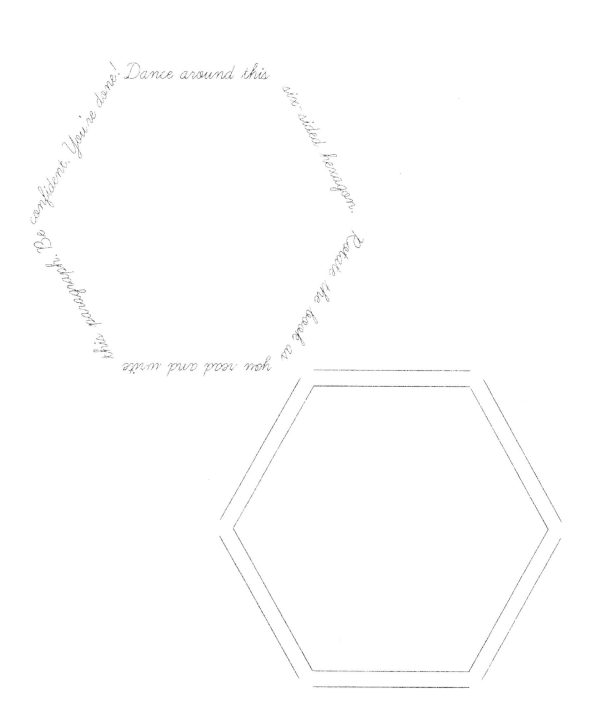

♫ 83 ♫

Spin your head round and round to read and write this paragraph. Where this paragraph ends, it once again begins:

If words could be your undoing, they would look something like this heart. I love this heart-shaped paragraph.

Contemplate the infinite wonders of a paragraph shaped like the infinity symbol. Where does it start and where does it end? That cycle is the first step toward decoding this.

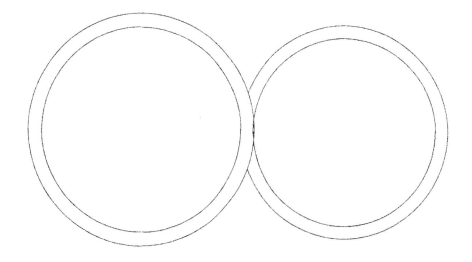

Part 6 Rewrite Print in Cursive

Part 6 Instructions: Rewrite these paragraphs in cursive handwriting on the blank lines below. Refer to pages 5-6 if you need help remembering what the cursive alphabet looks like. Check your answers at the back of the book.

Working out with your best friend can give you a little extra motivation. Choose a fun workout that you both enjoy. Fuel up with a protein shake of your favorite flavor.

Note: You should have enough room below to skip every other line.

_____

_____

_____

_____

_____

_____

What is your favorite type of music? Do you enjoy hip-hop, rock 'n' roll, rap, R & B, jazz, blues, classical, Latin, or something else? Who is your favorite artist? What is your favorite band? What is your favorite song? Do you prefer to listen to the radio, satellite, compact disc, M P 3 file, old-fashioned record, or something else?

_____
_____
_____
_____
_____
_____
_____
_____
_____
_____
_____

Imagine if you just received a million dollars! How much would be left after paying taxes? What would you do with the rest? Would you donate some to charity? Would you share with family or friends? Would you keep enough for yourself? Would you save it and just live off the interest? Would you start a business?

If you are hungry for outlandish fried foods, the State Fair is the place to get them. They are frying everything from Kool-Aid to bubblegum. You can load up on fat and carbs. Imagine eating a fried ice-cream cheeseburger, and then ordering deep-fried milk and cookies on a stick for dessert. Some people call these wild and crazy dishes "joke food."

_____

_____

_____

_____

_____

_____

_____

_____

_____

_____

_____

Some dogs can skateboard better than people. They star in many videos shown on YouTube. Pugs and bulldogs have a lower center of gravity, and are often seen skateboarding alongside their trainer. Dogs can surf, too. An annual surfing competition for dogs is held at Huntington Beach, California. Who will be the top dog?

Did you know that the first known motorized car race in the United States of America was held in Chicago, Illinois on Thanksgiving Day in 1895? It took the winner nearly eight hours to travel the length of the fifty-four mile course. The winner averaged a little more than seven miles per hour. Prize money for first place was five thousand dollars.

This is the first sentence of this paragraph. When a sentence refers to itself, it is called self-reference. This whole paragraph was written in the spirit of self-reference. This middle sentence feels neglected. What is this question asking? Unfortunately, this isn't the answer to that question. This is the final sentence of this paragraph.

It can be fun to make up words (but don't get upset if nobody else understands them). Jxqz could be a futuristic form of jazz. Wookisooki could be a newly discovered, adorable forest creature. Pizzagne could be a pizza topped with lasagna. Rhinopotamus could be a hippopotamus with a horn. What words would you make up?

Travel the world. (If you can't really go to these places, visit by using your imagination or reading about them.) Visit Stonehenge in England, the Eiffel Tower in Paris, the Colosseum in Rome, the ancient pyramids in Egypt, the Taj Mahal in India, the Great Wall of China, the Sydney Opera House in Australia, and the Galapagos Islands in Ecuador.

Have a lucky day. Find a lucky penny or four-leaf clover.

Or help make your own luck by preparing well, feeling

confident, staying calm when things don't go as planned,

and applying your problem-solving skills when they are

needed. Or make any day seem better by having a positive

outlook and making the most of whatever comes your way.

_____

_____

_____

_____

_____

_____

_____

_____

_____

_____

Halloween can involve more than just costumes. You and your friends can dress up like zombies and have a zombie race. You can wear vampire costumes and see who can suck the juice out of an orange the quickest. Dress up like werewolves on a full moon and have a howling contest. Witches can take part in a rotten stew contest.

What is your favorite restaurant? Do you like hamburgers, pizza, vegetarian dishes, salads, sandwiches, steak, chicken, ribs, stuffed peppers, spaghetti with meatballs, macaroni and cheese, lasagna, tacos, burritos, tamales, nachos, noodles, fried wontons, egg rolls, tempura, sushi, falafel, biryani, or something else? Or all of the above?

What is your favorite dessert? Do you like ice-cream, cake, cupcakes, popsicles, candy, cookies, muffins, pie, sundae, or another kind of dessert? What is your favorite flavor of ice-cream? Is it chocolate, vanilla, strawberry, or one of many other flavors? What is your favorite kind of pie? Is it apple, peach, lemon meringue, pecan, or another kind?

Once upon a time, it was a dark and stormy night. A princess was in distress. A knight in shining armor set out to save her. The princess was trapped in the tallest tower of a castle. The knight battled a fire-breathing dragon. The knight rescued the princess. They lived happily ever after. This story is so cliché. Don't like it? Rewrite it!

Part 7 Creative Writing Exercises

Part 7 Instructions: These creative writing prompts are designed to offer practice composing and writing sentences in cursive handwriting. If you forget how to write a letter of the alphabet in cursive, refer to pages 5-6.

1. If you could go back in history, what time frame would you like to visit? Why?

2. If you could star in any movie (old or new), which star and movie would you choose? Explain why you chose this movie and star.

3. Describe what you would do and change if you were President for one day. Why?

_____

_____

_____

_____

_____

_____

_____

_____

_____

_____

_____

_____

_____

_____

_____

_____

_____

_____

_____

_____

_____

_____

4. What super power would you like to have? How would you use it?

_____

_____

_____

_____

_____

_____

_____

_____

_____

_____

_____

_____

_____

_____

_____

_____

_____

_____

_____

5. If you could invent something (anything you want) to make your life easier, what would it be? Why?

_____

_____

_____

_____

_____

_____

_____

_____

_____

_____

_____

_____

_____

_____

_____

_____

_____

_____

_____

_____

_____

6. Would you be able to survive a day without using any electronic devices? What would it be like not to listen to music, watch television, or use your phone?

7. What is the nicest thing someone has ever told you? How did it make you feel? Have you repaid the favor (or have you paid it forward)? Explain.

8. Describe what inspires you.

_____
_____
_____
_____
_____
_____
_____
_____
_____
_____
_____
_____
_____
_____
_____
_____
_____
_____
_____
_____
_____
_____

9. What do you think will be up and coming trends in the next ten years?

_____
_____
_____
_____
_____
_____
_____
_____
_____
_____
_____
_____
_____
_____
_____
_____
_____
_____
_____
_____
_____

10. Describe the most adventuresome day you have ever experienced.

_____

_____

_____

_____

_____

_____

_____

_____

_____

_____

_____

_____

_____

_____

_____

_____

_____

_____

_____

_____

_____

11. What has been the hardest lesson you have learned? How has it affected you?

_____

_____

_____

_____

_____

_____

_____

_____

_____

_____

_____

_____

_____

_____

_____

_____

_____

_____

_____

_____

12. Who has been the most influential person in your life?
Explain how this person has been influential.

_____
_____
_____
_____
_____
_____
_____
_____
_____
_____
_____
_____
_____
_____
_____
_____
_____
_____
_____
_____
_____

13 Describe the first memory that you can remember.

_____

_____

_____

_____

_____

_____

_____

_____

_____

_____

_____

_____

_____

_____

_____

_____

_____

_____

_____

_____

_____

_____

_____

14. Do you think things are getting better or worse in our society? Explain why.

15. How do you see the town or city you live in ten years from now?

_____

_____

_____

_____

_____

_____

_____

_____

_____

_____

_____

_____

_____

_____

_____

_____

_____

_____

_____

_____

_____

_____

16. Describe an ideal summer getaway.

17. If your dreams could come true, what would happen?

_____
_____
_____
_____
_____
_____
_____
_____
_____
_____
_____
_____
_____
_____
_____
_____
_____
_____
_____
_____
_____
_____
_____

18. If you had a robot that could do anything for a day, what would you program it to do?

19. Write a short story.

20. Write a letter to a friend or relative. When you finish, copy your letter onto a separate sheet of lined paper and send it in the mail. Won't they be surprised to receive a special letter from you written in cursive handwriting?

Answers to Part 6

Page 87:

Working out with your best friend can give you a little extra motivation. Choose a fun workout that you both enjoy. Fuel up with a protein shake of your favorite flavor.

Page 88:

What is your favorite type of music? Do you enjoy hip-hop, rock 'n' roll, rap, R & B, jazz, blues, classical, Latin, or something else? Who is your favorite artist? What is your favorite band? What is your favorite song? Do you prefer to listen to the radio, satellite, compact disc, MP3 file, old-fashioned record, or something else?

Page 89:

Imagine if you just received a million dollars! How much would be left after paying taxes? What would you do with the rest? Would you donate some to charity? Would you share with family or friends? Would you keep enough for yourself? Would you save it and just live off the interest? Would you start a business?

Page 90:

If you are hungry for outlandish fried foods, the State Fair is the place to get them. They are frying everything from Kool-Aid to bubblegum. You can load up on fat and carbs. Imagine eating a fried ice-cream cheeseburger, and then ordering deep-fried milk and cookies on a stick for dessert. Some people call these wild and crazy dishes "joke food."

Page 91:

Some dogs can skateboard better than people. They star in many videos shown on YouTube. Pugs and bulldogs have a lower center of gravity, and are often seen skateboarding alongside their trainer. Dogs can surf, too. An annual surfing competition for dogs is held at Huntington Beach, California. Who will be the top dog?

Page 92:

Did you know that the first known motorized car race in the United States of America was held in Chicago, Illinois on Thanksgiving Day in 1895? It took the winner nearly eight hours to travel the length of the fifty-four mile course. The winner averaged a little more than seven miles per hour. Prize money for first place was five thousand dollars.

Page 93:

This is the first sentence of this paragraph. When a sentence refers to itself, it is called self-reference. This whole paragraph was written in the spirit of self-reference. This middle sentence feels neglected. What is this question asking? Unfortunately, this isn't the answer to that question. This is the final sentence of this paragraph.

Page 94:

It can be fun to make up words (but don't get upset if nobody else understands them). Jxqz could be a futuristic form of jazz. Wookisooki could be a newly discovered, adorable forest creature. Pizzagne could be a pizza topped with lasagna. Rhinopotamus could be a hippopotamus with a horn. What words would you make up?

Page 95:

Travel the world. (If you can't really go to these places, visit by using your imagination or reading about them.) Visit Stonehenge in England, the Eiffel Tower in Paris, the Colosseum in Rome, the ancient pyramids in Egypt, the Taj Mahal in India, the Great Wall of China, the Sydney Opera House in Australia, and the Galapagos Islands in Ecuador.

Page 96:

Have a lucky day. Find a lucky penny or four-leaf clover. Or help make your own luck by preparing well, feeling confident, staying calm when things don't go as planned, and applying your problem-solving skills when they are needed. Or make any day seem better by having a positive outlook and making the most of whatever comes your way.

Page 97:

Halloween can involve more than just costumes. You and your friends can dress up like zombies and have a zombie race. You can wear vampire costumes and see who can suck the juice out of an orange the quickest. Dress up like werewolves on a full moon and have a howling contest. Witches can take part in a rotten stew contest.

Page 98:

What is your favorite restaurant? Do you like hamburgers, pizza, vegetarian dishes, salads, sandwiches, steak, chicken, ribs, stuffed peppers, spaghetti with meatballs, macaroni and cheese, lasagna, tacos, burritos, tamales, nachos, noodles, fried wontons, egg rolls, tempura, sushi, falafel, biryani, or something else? Or all of the above?

Page 99:

What is your favorite dessert? Do you like ice-cream, cake, cupcakes, popsicles, candy, cookies, muffins, pie, sundae, or another kind of dessert? What is your favorite flavor of ice-cream? Is it chocolate, vanilla, strawberry, or one of many other flavors? What is your favorite kind of pie? Is it apple, peach, lemon meringue, pecan, or another kind?

Page 100:

Once upon a time, it was a dark and stormy night. A princess was in distress. A knight in shining armor set out to save her. The princess was trapped in the tallest tower of a castle. The knight battled a fire-breathing dragon. The knight rescued the princess. They lived happily ever after. This story is so cliché. Don't like it? Rewrite it!

Julie Harper Books

wackysentences.com

amazon.com/author/julieharper

Printing Practice:

Printing Practice Handwriting Workbook for Girls / Boys

Tongue Twisters Printing Practice Writing Workbook

Print Uppercase and Lowercase Letters, Words, and Silly Phrases

Print Wacky Sentences: First and Second Grade Writing Practice Workbook

Cursive Handwriting:

Butterfly Cursive Handwriting Practice Workbook

Flower Cursive Handwriting Practice Workbook

Save the Earth Cursive Handwriting Practice Workbook

Letters, Words, and Silly Phrases Handwriting Workbook (Reproducible)

Wacky Sentences Handwriting Workbook (Reproducible)

Cursive Handwriting Workbook for Girls / Boys / Teens

Spooky Cursive Handwriting Practice Workbook

Friendship Cursive Handwriting Practice Workbook

Reading & Writing:

Reading Comprehension for Girls

Read Wacky Sentences Basic Reading Comprehension Workbook

Wacky Creative Writing Assignments Workbook

70422729R00073

Made in the USA
Middletown, DE
13 April 2018